BREAD OF LIFE

LYNN KRAJCI

WESTBOW
PRESS®
A DIVISION OF THOMAS NELSON
& ZONDERVAN

WestBow Press books may be ordered through booksellers or by contacting:

WestBow Press
A Division of Thomas Nelson & Zondervan
1663 Liberty Drive
Bloomington, IN 47403
www.westbowpress.com
844-714-3454

Scripture quotations marked (ESV) are from the ESV® Bible (The Holy Bible,
English Standard Version®), copyright © 2001 by Crossway, a publishing ministry
of Good News Publishers. Used by permission. All rights reserved.

Scriptures marked NASB are taken from the NEW AMERICAN STANDARD BIBLE®, Copyright © 1960,
1962, 1963, 1968, 1971, 1972, 1973, 1975, 1977, 1995 by The Lockman Foundation. Used by permission.

ISBN: 979-8-3850-0457-7 (sc)
ISBN: 979-8-3850-0458-4 (e)

Library of Congress Control Number: 2023914601

Print information available on the last page.

WestBow Press rev. date: 08/24/2023

CONTENTS

BY THE EDGE OF A PRAYER

When life's mountains are to high to climb

And its oceans are too wide

When I am overwhelmed with grief

When the cliffs are too steep

And the waters too deep

I find myself holding on to You

I'm holding on by the edge of a prayer

and I'm longing for You to be there

When a traumatic day comes crashing through

I'm holding on my God to You

I'm holding on by the edge of a prayer

And I'm hoping my LORD that you will be there

To hear my mournful cry and my tearful sorrow

When I am out of my own strength and there's none to borrow

I'm holding on my God to You, by the edge of a prayer

Oh, in times of heart wrenching despair

My LORD, I'm holding on to You

When life's mountains are too high to climb

When oceans are too wide

When the cliffs are too steep

And the waters are too deep

I'm reaching, reaching out to You

By the edge of a prayer

In times of heart wrenching despair

When I am unable to comprehend

I'm holding on my God, holding on to You again

Because I believe that You deeply care

So, I'm holding on to You, by the edge of a prayer.

LYNN KRAJCI

BE STILL

Throughout my life whenever troubles came

I heard a whisper again and again

The voice softly spoke, "Be still."

When darkness fell and doors slammed shut

When losses piled and devastation crushed

I heard the whisper

When sadness mounted

When blackness surrounded

The voice abounded, "Be still."

When pain was weighty

And troubles unabated

When I saw no hope ahead

When sorrow endured without end

I heard the voice again, "Be still."

I did not understand, so I slowed, I tarried

Who was this voice that my burden carried?

The voice was faint, but the message grew clear

"Be still, be calm, for I am here."

Then suddenly my heart was freed

Be still indeed! I understood

This was no ordinary plea

This was the voice of the One who bled and died for me!

"Fear not!" He now shouted, "For you are mine!

I will comfort you beyond the edge of all time!"

No enemy shall overtake you

No danger can await you

If you have heard the whisper divine

The voice that says, "Be still, you are mine."

He will comfort and console you

Where He leads, I will go

When He defends, no one can contend

When He calls, I will hear

When He whispers, I will always draw near

For I am quieted, just as He calmed the sea

He has surely entered and quieted me

He once whispered, but now He shouts

His voice much louder, His message dear

And I am forever still, while He is forever near.

LYNN KRAJCI

English Standard Version Psalm 46:10 "**Be still and Know that I am God.**"

BELIEVE

All things are possible if you believe

Still, I ask You Lord, "Help my unbelief!"

If I believe in Him, as He wills, it will be done

And if I trust in Him, it will become

As I look to Him and to His Son

Often, I have prayed, and You've replied

Sometimes my prayer's refused, and I ask why

Sometimes I see what You have taught

Then I understand what You have sought

When You've not answered my way

I continue to hope and continue to pray

Often, I have asked, and You've replied

You've healed, You've protected, You've not denied

Sometimes I request of You and there is silence

I wait patiently in full compliance

I know I will hear from You in Your good timing

I know You will answer me when I am pining

All things are possible if you believe

Still, I ask You Lord, "Help my unbelief!"

If I believe in Him, as He wills, it will be done

And if I trust in Him, it will become

As I look to Him and to His Son

You say, "Yes," You say, "No," and You say, "Wait"

But Lord, Your answer is never wrong and never late

You always bless, You are never slow

Your purpose is for our wisdom to grow

All things are possible if you believe

If you believe in Him, as He wills, it will be done

And if you trust in Him, you will overcome

If you look to the only, the holy,

the solely, Everlasting One.

LYNN KRAJCI

English Standard Version Mark 9:24 Immediately the father of the child cried out and said, "I believe, help my unbelief."

DO WHAT DAVID DID

When you are weak and in a vulnerable state

When you are old and walking with feeble gait

Do not feel forgotten, indifferent or discouraged

But be greatly encouraged

And do what David did

Trust in the faithful God

The sturdy bridge

Who takes us over rough waters

The solid God of the martyrs

When you feel defeated and alone

Do not despair, give up or groan

Do not shrink in fear or faint

Do not lose heart and seek complaint

But do what David did

Look to our Rock of Refuge

Look to our Deliverer, King of the Angels

Proclaim His glorious deeds

To the next generation

Show them where He leads

Tell them of your unbounded adoration

Resound of His eternal salvation

And never from the Word of God backdown

For His Word, you know, is eternally profound

Do not fear the consequence

Always speak His Word with reverence

Then when you are old you will have no regret

You'll be fearless in His righteousness

You'll be hopeful in His promises

In His works wonderful and marvelous

So do what David did

Continually praise our God

Trust in the Rock of Refuge

The Deliverer, the King of Angels

Teach your sons and daughters

About the bridge that takes us over rough waters

Of the Rock of Refuge

The King of the Angels

And do what David did.

LYNN KRAJCI

English Standard Version Psalm 71:3 "Be to me a **rock of refuge**, to which I may continually come; you have given the command to save me, for you are my **rock** and my fortress."

The LORD is my rock and my fortress and my **deliverer**, my God, my rock, in whom I take refuge, my shield, and the horn of my salvation, my stronghold.

DO YOU CARE FOR ME?

To the God who made the universe

Who set its laws in motion

And set the rules for the tides of the oceans

Do You care for me?

To the God who tells the flowers when to bloom

And gave the bird's heart its tune

Who causes them to take flight in the heavens

Who causes the human heart to question

Do You care for me?

To the God who made the caterpillar take colorful wing

Who gave the bee its terrible sting

Who sets the sky ablaze when the sun goes down

And upon its rising bathes the world in light that surrounds

Do You care for me?

To You I bow

Because I know You do

But I know not why

And I know not how.

LYNN KRAJCI

A PRAYER FOR THE CHILDREN

Though they believe that You are sovereign
And though we have taught them
That You will always pardon

Life is a difficult road

Lord, comfort and protect the children
For they know not what they do
As sometimes they will stray and will lose sight of You

Though they believe
There will be times when they feel forgotten
These feelings they have are not that uncommon

Life is a difficult road.

When doubtful from sadness
When feeling defeat
Forgive them and guide them
When they have the need

Show them forgiveness
Teach them to love
Make them Your witnesses
Reveal from above

Let them be wise, protect from deceit

Give them clear eyes, don't let them retreat

Because life is a difficult road.

When losses are hard, and mountains are steep

When they are old, and their bodies grow weak

Don't let them be angry or feel incomplete

Let them lean on You Lord remaining holy and meek

Lord comfort and protect the children

For they know not what they do

And sometimes they stray and lose sight of You

Though they believe

You are sovereign

Though they believe

You will always pardon

Protect the children

For life is a difficult road.

LYNN KRAJCI

FOREVER LOVING YOU

Lord, I'm forever loving You

You come to me when it's quiet and I'm alone

You come to me when I'm silent and all my words have flown

You comfort me when trouble invades and I'm afraid

Lord, I'm forever loving You

You're my hope through the darkness

When people are cruel and heartless

I long for You to take me home

To the place where you ascended to Your throne

To that place where goodness and gladness are sown

Where there is no reason to ever fear

Or to shed even a single sorrowful tear

Lord, I'm forever loving You

You come to me when it's quiet and I'm all alone

You come to me when I'm silent and my words have flown

You comfort me when trouble invades and I'm afraid

You are my hope in the darkness

And when life delivers its hardest

Lord, I'm forever loving You

Someday, You will come I know
And take me to the place where you ascended Your throne
Where there is no reason to ever fear
Or to shed even a single sorrowful tear

Lord, You're my hope in the darkness
Someday when this world I've departed
I will shed tears, not of sorrow, but of joy
As all cause of fear, You will destroy
All reason for sadness will vanish

And I will be in Your glorious presence
Enjoying Your very essence
Forever exhilarated, forever elated
Forever desiring You
Forever inclined toward Your truth

And Lord, forever loving You

LYNN KRAJCI

GATHER AND LISTEN

Gather and listen, I will tell you the story

Of the Son of Man who will come in power and great glory

It will be after the tribulation of those days

When the Son of Man comes to take us away

He will gather us from the four winds

All who have repented and are forgiven their sins

On that day the Lord will raise His own to meet Him in the air

Where we will gather to declare,

"Glory to the Lamb of God our King

Who comes to rectify all things!"

Every eye will see Him like a lightning blaze

And on that day, many will be afraid

A time when the powers of heaven will be shaken

When the sun will be darkened, the stars falling

The nations on that day will mourn

As they realize they are accountable to the Lord

While they feel great sorrow and fear

The elect will rejoice for our Lord has appeared

Our Messiah and Savior has drawn near

For those who believe there will be gladness and glorious kismet

For those who have not believed, only sadness and regret

On that day, heaven will open, and He will ride on a white horse

He will come to rule and enforce

He is the One, faithful and true

He will deal out to all nations whatever their due

He will judge and wage war

He is worthy, for in Him is no flaw

His eyes like flames of fire

Nations will tremble before His fierce ire

Man's strongholds He will tear down

And He will fight with the sword of His mouth

A name is written on Him that no one else knows

All this will occur when the trumpet blows

With a rod of iron, He will strike the nations

With a rod of iron, He will rule and take action swift and brazen

He is clothed in a robe dipped in blood

He is followed by His heavenly army on white horses above

His fame all the earth knew and heard

His famous and righteous name is the Word

He treads the winepress of God's wrath

On that day when He straightens the crooked paths

On His robe and thigh, a name is written

It is "King of Kings and Lord of Lords"

He will fight the battle with His mighty sword

The kings of the earth and their foolish armies will gather for war against Him

He will defeat them, they will surely come to a swift and final end

The Beast and False Prophet who deceive those who receive the "Mark of the Beast"

Will surely meet with sound defeat

At their fatal doom

For they will be thrown in the eternal fire that consumes

So, gather and listen to the story of the Son of Man

Who will come with power and great glory to fulfill His imminent plan

On that day of war and wedding feast

The day of the Lord, the day of relief

The day when our Lord comes to make the crooked paths straight

The day when our Lord comes to both forgive and forsake

And on that day, we will say,

"Praise to our God all you who fear Him both small and great

For He has come and made the way straight!"

On that day crowns will be laid at His feet

For He is so worthy and His victory so sweet

And we will sing, "Hallelujah, for the Lord Almighty reigns!

He has come and will forever remain

Hallelujah all heaven and earth is His domain

Righteousness and justice have come

And God's Eternal Kingdom has finally begun!"

So, gather and listen to the true story of the Son of Man

Who will soon come in power and glory grand

And pray that you will be among the crowd

Who meets Him in the cloud

So, pay close attention, please gather and listen.

LYNN KRAJCI

Psalm 33:5 He loves righteousness and justice; the earth is full of the steadfast love of the LORD.

ESV Matthew 13:26 And then they will see THE SON OF MAN COMING IN CLOUDS with great power and glory.

NASB Matthew 24: 27 For just as the lightning comes from the east and flashes as far as the west, so will the coming of the Son of Man be.

NASB Matthew 24: 29 Immediately after the tribulation of those days shall the sun be darkened, and the moon shall not give her light, and the stars shall fall from heaven, and the powers of the heavens shall be shaken:

NASB Matthew 24:30 And then the sign of the Son of Man will appear in the sky, and then all the tribes of the earth will mourn, and they will see the SON OF MAN COMING ON THE CLOUDS OF THE SKY with power and great glory.

NASB Matthew 24:31 And He will send forth His angels with A GREAT TRUMPET BLAST, and THEY WILL GATHER TOGETHER His elect from the four winds, from one end of the sky to the other.

Mark 13:24 But in those days, after that tribulation, the sun shall be darkened, and the moon shall not give her lght,

NASB Mark 13;27 And then He will send forth the angels and will gather together His elect from the four winds, from the end of the earth to the end of heaven.

ESV Luke 21:27 And then they will see the Son of Man coming in a cloud with power and great glory.

Revelation 4:10 …the twenty-four elders will fall down before Him who sits on the throne, and they will worship Him who lives forever and ever, and will cast their crowns before the throne, saying,

ESV Revelation 19:6 Then I heard *something* like the voice of a great multitude and like the sound of many waters, and like the sound of mighty peals of thunder, saying, "Hallelujah! For the Lord our God, the Almighty, reigns.

IF GOD IS FOR US

If God is for us, who can be against us?

Who or what can boast of being strong enough?

The most ferocious winter storm?

An army charging with all human scorn?

God did not spare His Son, but delivered Him up for us

His Son willingly died, so in Him we can put our trust

What can conquer a love so robust?

Some command or fatal decree?

Or any force of any degree?

Can a thousand lightning strikes or rattlesnake bites?

Who can separate us from the love of Christ?

Surely there is nothing on earth or in heaven above

That can part us from Him or from His love

Not even persecution, tribulation or famine can stand

Nothing can remove us from His loving hand

No one and nothing can overcome God's grand plan

God justifies and no one can condemn or refute

God reconciles and no one can contend or rebuke

So, what can separate us from the love of God?

Not angels, nor principalities or an iron rod

Nothing will separate us from the love of God

Not even death or life, nor depth or height

For our God is the God immutable

And His Word is the Word indisputable

He fights with His invincible sword

His ways, no one can even begin to abort

In all things we overwhelmingly conquer through Him

We overthrow, we triumph and subdue through Him

For our God is the Almighty God who defeated death and sin

He is God of heaven and earth and our battle He did surely win.

LYNN KRAJCI

ESV Romans 8 31-39 What then shall we say to these things? If God is for us, who can be[i] against us? He who did not spare his own Son but gave him up for us all, how will he not also with him graciously give us all things? Who shall bring any charge against God's elect? It is God who justifies. Who is to condemn? Christ Jesus is the one who died—more than that, who was raised—who is at the right hand of God, who indeed is interceding for us.[j] Who shall separate us from the love of Christ? Shall tribulation, or distress, or persecution, or famine, or nakedness, or danger, or sword? As it is written,"For your sake we are being killed all the day long; we are regarded as sheep to be slaughtered." No, in all these things we are more than conquerors through him who loved us. For I am sure that neither death nor life, nor angels nor rulers, nor things present nor things to come, nor powers, nor height nor depth, nor anything else in all creation, will be able to separate us from the love of God in Christ Jesus our Lord..

LORD, WE KNOW

Lord, didn't know what glorious was

Until we were down and looking up

Didn't know what wonder was

Until we saw Your love

Lord, can't believe

You left Your heavenly seat

To sacrifice an aroma so sweet

Father, we didn't know what wonder was

Until You revealed Your Son

Lord didn't see what sacrifice was

Until we saw Your blood

Didn't know what beauty was

Until we felt Your love

Lord, didn't know wondrous

Didn't know marvelous

Didn't know glorious

But now we are looking up

To the One who drank the cup

And Lord we know, Lord we know.

LYNN KRAJCI

MAKING IT SO

A hint of pink breaks through the winter clouds

Touching the snow-draped branches that surround

While the sharp chill of crisp winter air blows

Melting drops of snow form ringlets in the half-frozen stream below

Hinting at Winter's slowly growing fear

That Spring's grand, and elegant entrance is drawing near.

I sit beside the still water, feeling the cold wet snow

As it soaks through my well-worn blue jean coat

And I think about the God who makes it all so.

The beauty of this damp frosty morning and all the dazzling snow

And the senses that cause me to see, feel, hear and know

And again, I think of the noble God who made it so,

The voices of robins and song sparrows

Reach hearts and ears shooting their melodic arrows through the cold

And I smile, as I drift away to dream awhile

Not understanding the ecstasy of this lofty mystery

Now the hue of pink spreads across white clouds

Touching the snow-cloaked trees that surround

While the sharp chill of winter breeze blows

Drops of melting snow form ringlets in the half-frozen stream below

Hinting of Winter's slowly yielding fear

of Spring's grand and graceful entrance drawing near

I sit still beside the stream feeling the cold wet snow

as it soaks through my old blue-jean coat

And consider the lofty God who made it so

Remembering the beauty of that cool and quiet morn so long ago

And the senses that caused me to see, feel, hear and know

I am greatly moved, and thank the God who made it all so...

LYNN KRAJCI

MY GOD, MY LIVING GOD

I need You when things are clear cut

I need You when I'm about to plummet

I don't know how I'd get by

If I didn't know You were alive

My God, my living God

I need You when storms are thrashing

I need You when life's walls are cracking

I don't know how I'd survive

Without knowing You are alive

My God, my living God

I need You now and forever

I bow down to You, I surrender

My God, my living God

I need You in the morning and in the night

When clouds block out the daylight

I need You when things are clear cut

I need You when I'm about to plummet

I don't know how I'd survive

If I didn't know You were alive

My God, my living God

When storms are thrashing

When life's walls are cracking

Don't know how I'd be sound

Without knowing You're around

My God, my living God.

LYNN KRAJCI

NO GREATER LOVE

God shows Himself in many ways

In the mountains high, in a fire's blaze or a summer day

In the lion's roar, in the children born

In the dog's wagging tail

In the spray of the great blue whale

In the ocean waves, in the bear's dark cave

He has not left us in the dark

He's made it clear from the very start

In morning haze over a quiet lake

In a child's gaze, in a slithering snake

In the flower's bloom, in the peacock's plume

God shows Himself when a person prays

But God shows Himself in other ways

In the falling rain, in the rolling plains

In the autumn leaves or an ocean breeze

In the fish of the water, in the birds that fly

In the playful otter, or a sunset sky

God has made Himself known

In all these things His love is shown

But also, in that He saved the lost

We see Him most clearly through the cross

We were blinded by the enemy
But now we look up, wake up and see
Rejoice that He was sent
Rejoice that He died then rose again

He didn't leave us in the shadows
Nor did He leave us as a land fallow
He sowed the seed, He brought the rain
Glory to His holy name
That though we die we live again
And there is no greater friend
Praise, for His heavenly kiss
Praise for there is no greater love than this.

LYNN KRAJCI

ODE TO THE GOOD PASTOR

He speaks with persuasive eloquence

To an assorted and attentive audience

He must tread lightly, yet boldly still

And surely he must convey the Father's will

He must maintain the peace of course

Yet he must be careful about the cost

He desires to please the Lord

But He also must deal with the difficult sorts

He must remain calm though he wants to scream

Carefully walking that line in-between

Honor the good pastor, the shepherd of the sheep

For he is there in our joy and there when we weep

The pastor feeds his hungry lambs

Leading them through God's Word the best that he can

He must feed his sheep taking faithful leaps

Honor the good pastor

Who is always testing the wind

Not knowing the mood it is blowing in

Have mercy on the good pastor

Who strives not to offend

For there are always those who choose to contend

And he shows great restraint when the sheep bleat their many complaints

Spare the good pastor

Who leads you along the narrow way

Protects from wolves his lambs who go stray

Love the good shepherd who guides his sheep

For I know, over you, he loses much sleep

He leads his flock to places of good forage

And guards your souls with great courage

Pray for the good pastor for he is responsible

His climb appears insurmountable

And for your souls he stands most accountable

Honor the good pastor whose days are sacrificial

Know that his efforts are surely not superficial

His enemies are many, like wolves lying in wait to pounce on the sheep

He must remain wary while a great harvest he loyally reaps

God bless the good pastor

Honor him, praise him, encourage him all

For, when necessary, it is he who must stand in the gap and take the fall

Favor him, respect him and love him please

For he it is that sows God's bountiful seed

Care for him for he guards your souls

Protects from predators and must play many roles

He speaks with eloquence to his attentive and assorted audience

He must tread lightly, yet boldly still

So, honor the good pastor who serves with multiple skills

Care for him and appreciate all that he does

For he acts, I assure you, with the Spirit of God's tender love.

LYNN KRAJCI

JUST OPEN UP YOUR EYES

The truth is blowing in the wind
It is written across the sky
You need not search for it
Only open up your eyes

The Lord's revelation
Is seen in His creation

Open up your eyes

Flowers unfold at springtime's sight
Feathered birds' newborns take flight

At sunrise an array of color
Splashes its hue across the summer

Winter freezes the world in snow
Giving life a purifying glow

Autumn comes and trees begin to sing
They create a wondrous scene
Colors burst forth and abound
Awakened to the fact that God surrounds

The Lord's revelation

Is seen in His creation

Open up your eyes

His truth is written in the autumn breeze

In the winter freeze

In the summer sun

When spring flowers have sprung

The truth is blowing in the wind

It is written across the sky

You need not search hard for it

Just open up your eyes.

LYNN KRAJCI

PRAISE HIM

The human being has a strange mind

We are not the same as any other kind

We can be the cruelest of the creatures

Waging war is one of our most notable features

We understand what the others cannot ever

For as human beings we are the most clever

We calculate the numbers flawlessly

We invent complex technology

We build toys that entertain us

And tall skyscrapers able to contain much

It seems there is nothing that constrains us

Humankind has a strange mind

We are not the same as any other kind

We cannot run like the antelope or leap as a cat

But we can thoroughly inform of the scientific facts

We are entranced by a rainy spring day

Or by the autumn leaves' colorful array

We are in awe of the daylily's bloom

Or the lovely scent of a flower's perfume

And we marvel with delight

When an eagle spreads his wings in flight

Yet we also reason, we can figure things out

And for all these attributes, how do we account?

Humankind is a strange being

We are not like any other thing

We are cruel, we are tender

We are shrewd with no equal contender

Yet to nature's beauty we often surrender

Consider everything about man

Our strengths, our abilities

And all that we think we understand

From where come our abilities?

From where our instability?

Why is the human mind so strange and so marvelous?

Why so kind and yet unscrupulous?

Made in God's image, we are very good

Finding and choosing sin, we act not as we should

In His image we are made to delight at the flight of a bird of prey

And we are touched by the beauty of a summer's day

From where then comes our evil bend?

From where our blind decline?

We have been told it is the dark enemy within

Our terrible tendency to embrace sin

Yet we are so wonderfully made
So, I have to ask, can mankind be saved?

Yes! For there is hope in the Friend of Man
The Defender, the Conqueror and King,
And I am glad
For He has given us everything

So, praise Him who is worthy
Praise Him for His mercy
And thank Him for His grace
He intercedes in heaven, He has won the insurmountable race
He is the Almighty's only begotten Son
The Creator, the Holy, the Most High Exquisite One.

LYNN KRAJCI

NASB Genesis 9 :6 Whoever sheds the blood of man, by man shall his blood be shed, for God made man in his own image.

PSALM OF SALVATION

Lord, I know Your heart

How You desire all people to depart

From the sin that entraps them

And You're calling us to go

Even to the remote

Places of the earth

To leave traces of Your truth

For all that it's worth there

So, Lord we ask, and we plead

Be kind and be quick to spare

For Your glorious salvation

Was meant to be shared,

With all the world,

So let Your grace be unfurled

Let Your salvation be known

To every soul

Let it widely be shown

And shout it from the rooftops of all civilizations

Let them hear and accept Your gracious invitation

All the peoples from every tribe, tongue, and nation

Oh, that Your will might be known

To all human creation

Let us understand Your global intentions

Cause them to see the vastness of Your great love

And join us in singing Your awesome and wonderful psalm

Let us reap a broad and great harvest

Lift the people out of their deep darkness

Show them Your shining light

Allow them to understand what is truly right

Cause them to shed the terrors of the night

To see the ascending height of Your infinite love

Streaming down from heaven above

Save them, spare them, let them hear

Send us, move us, let us draw them near

Cause them to join us in reaching the rest

Please LORD hear our most earnest request

Add their voices to the psalm of salvation that we sing

and add them to the ever-growing voices

Grateful to our praiseworthy King.

LYNN KRAJCI

REJOICE

When your heart aches
And friends make promises they only intend to break
When morning after morning sorrow overflows your plate

I say, "Rejoice."

Death has entered too many times of late
Now alone, everyone's gone to their grave
Sadness penetrates even your inner safe place

And I say, "Rejoice."

All you know now is various shades of sorrow
And hope has left for all tomorrows
Life seems a foolish thing
And you can't understand why you've stayed so long
No one does what is right anymore

Even all you've ever done seems embedded in wrong
News headlines tear your heart in two
You're angry, you're fearful, you don't know what to do

And I say, "Rejoice!"

Hope is hanging by a weak and thin string

Now you're old and tired, you've got nothin' left to bring

But you see only darkness

And life's endless harshness

And you ask, "What am I living for?

More sadness and torrents of pain?

For what was I born?

And what have I to gain?"

I won't say that you're not seein' it right

I won't tell you that your pain's not in vain

I will only say, "Rejoice."

For there is One who is to come

Who has power to turn darkness to sun

He can change our sinful world

Causing blessed love to unfurl

On that day we will celebrate with unimaginable gladness

On that day He will put an end to all the terrible madness

For He touches and there is no turning back

For He heals and supplies all that you lack

He speaks and the universe obeys

He is able to remove all the sins that betray

He will not compromise with the world and its ways

He will reign and rule with a strong and sure hand

The enemy will flee at His slightest command

Death and sin will be gone at His mighty roar

Death and sin will be gone forevermore

"Rejoice!"

LYNN KRAJCI

SEEING YOU IN YOUR GRAND CREATION

I am hiking with that old walking stick

Following the stream around those mountain cliffs

A yellow leaf floats by until it is trapped by stones in the creek

And I decide to take a seat on a large rock nearby

I look up and only see the orange leaves of autumn and no sky

Moving ahead I see a deer drinking water

She tilts her head to ponder

I look at her in wonder

In a moment, she darts away

Deciding not to stay

Then I smile remembering the reason I have come so often

To see You Lord, in Your creation

I can see my breath as it hits cold air

It feels good to be cold this time of year

I tread along the path again

And the leaves begin to rustle in the wind

Then red, yellow, and orange they fall like rain

And I feel not at all alone, but as though You also came

You walk beside me as I hike this trail

And I watch a bird through the branches sail

I can see You Lord in the things You have made

I can hear You Lord in the bird's serenade

I love these woods; I'd come more often if I could

Because I feel You in the air

Because Your creation is everywhere

I walk ahead to a clearing where I see a deep blue sky

With a single white cloud floating by

I hear the sound of the water in the creek

In this place where beauty is so replete

I am thankful for all You've made for us

A breeze blows and my coat's collar I adjust

I smile again remembering the reason I had come

To see You Lord in Your creation

The leaves begin to rustle in the wind

As I tread along the path again

Then red, yellow and orange they fall like rain

And I feel I am not alone, but as though You also came

I am walking with that old walking stick

Following the stream around those mountain cliffs

And I smile remembering why I so often come

To see You Lord in Your grand creation.

LYNN KRAJCI

TO THE UNBELIEVER: THE MAN WHO SO LOVED YOU

I don't understand how you could see the Man

And not love Him as He loved you

Why are you not moved by His sacrifice?

Why do you not see the wonder of the Christ?

He has taken death, sin and pain

And though this truth remains

You don't see, you won't see

The gentle Lamb was slain for me and you

Why don't you see this great truth?

It is right before your eyes

But still, you refuse to realize

I don't understand how you could see the Man

And not take hold of his blood-stained hand

He suffered for our sins

He said, "Knock and I'll let you in."

Why are you not moved by His dying in your stead?

Why will you not see that He and only He is your closest friend?

Ask and it will be given, knock and the door will be opened

Listen closely to the wisdom He has spoken

He has reached out to you, so take His hand

Or help me to understand

Why you are unwilling to love the man

Who so loved you.

LYNN KRAJCI

KJV Revelation 3:20 Behold, I stand at the door, and knock: if any man hear my voice, and open the door, I will come in to him, and will sup with him, and he with me.

Revelation 5:12 Saying with a loud voice, Worthy is the Lamb that was slain to receive power, and riches, and wisdom, and strength, and honour, and glory, and blessing.

THE ALPHA AND OMEGA

In the beginning God created the earth and the heavens

Mountains, rolling hills, plains and deserts

Something had to come first from an infinite source

In order for the universe to take its course

All was formless and dark until God's Spirit hovered over the waters

And all things received their orders

God spoke and it came to be

In part it is clear, in part a mystery

God said, "Let there be light," and the sun appeared to volunteer

He said, "Let there be night," and the sun disappeared

He made dry land and gathered the seas

He commanded there be plants yielding seed

God made the trees that bear fruit

And made animals and man to reproduce

He also created the creatures of the oceans

And set the tides in their endless motion

He made man in His image

But He did not create him with the sin he committed

Man chose this way

And we live with the consequences to this very day

The results dark and sorrowful

Treacherous and deeply mournful

Our only hope is the Messiah and Lord

Who is the only One able to restore

Jesus Christ is His name

Only He can remove the sin and its stain

He was there in the beginning and created all things

He is our Lord God and our King

He is the beginning and the end

Our great Savior and friend

He died for us and for us He rose again

In the beginning He was the infinite source

He it was who ordered the universe to take its course

He spoke and everything was made

Because when He speaks, the universe obeys

When He forgives, it is done

When He permits, it is the certain outcome

He spoke and everything was made

Because when He speaks, the universe obeys.

LYNN KRAJCI

NASB Genesis 1:1-3 In the beginning God created the heavens and the earth. And the earth was formless and desolate emptiness, and darkness was over the [c]surface of the deep, and the Spirit of God was hovering over the [c]surface of the waters. Then God said, "[I]Let there be light"; and there was light.

NASB Genesis 1:9 Then God said, "Let the waters below the heavens be gathered into one place, and let the dry land appear"; and it was so.

NASB Genesis 1:11 Then God said, "Let the earth sprout vegetation, plants yieldin seed, *and* fruit trees on the earth bearing fruit according to their kind with seed in them"; and it was so.

NASB Genesis 1:27 So God created man in His own image, in the image of God He created him; male and female He created them.

NASB Mark 16:6 But he *said to them, "Do not be amazed; you are looking for Jesus the Nazarene, who has been crucified. He has risen; He is not here; see, *here is* the place where they laid Him.

WHEN WE RISE

When we rise

The deaf will hear

The dumb will talk

The lame will walk

The blind will see

And we will open our eyes to the King of Kings.

We shall rise on our wedding day

And the bride will say, "Hallelujah!"

The trumpet will be blown before us

That day of great joy will not elude or exclude us

And we will rise and say,

"Praise to Him,

For He is the reason we live again

Praise for His wedding gift--

Eternal life with eternal bliss!"

We shall rise

We shall rise on our wedding day

For death and sin have fled away

Death has retreated and sin has not succeeded

Love has won

Hate is finished, it is done

Sorrow and pain have fled from the presence of the Son.

When we rise

The deaf will hear

The dumb will talk

The lame will walk

The blind will see

On that day when we open our eyes to the King of Kings.

We will rise on our wedding day

And the bride will say, "Hallelujah!"

The trumpet will sound

And that great day will abound

With many souls--the wife of the husband--

The one and only Husband-King

Who we placed all our trust in.

When we rise

We will say,

"Hallelujah for the wedding day!"

When we open our eyes we will sing,

"Hallelujah to the King of Kings."

LYNN KRAJCI

NASB Revelation 19:7 Let's rejoice and be glad and give the glory to Him, because the marriage of the Lamb has come, and His bride has prepared herself."

NASB Matthew 11:5 *those who are* BLIND RECEIVE SIGHT and *those who* limp walk, *those* with leprosy are cleansed and *those who are* deaf hear, *the* dead are raised, and *the* POOR HAVE THE GOSPEL PREACHED TO THEM.

NASB Matthew 24:31 And He will send forth His angels with A GREAT TRUMPET BLAST, and THEY WILL GATHER TOGETHER His elect from the four winds, from one end of the sky to the other.

YOU MAKE MY HEART SING

The wonders of what you do, wash over me and through

My tears are stirred by the sights and sounds of what You have done

By Your goodness and mercy I am overcome

My Savior and King-my thirst for you unquenching

Your sacrifice for us heart wrenching

O resurrected King, You make my heart sing

The wonders of what You have done, wash over me and through

My tears are stirred by the sights and sounds of all You've done

By Your glory and grace I am overcome

Revere His holy name, remember why He came

Let the Spirit dance, let the heart sing

And remember with gladness that He alone will reign

Look forward to the peace and prosperity that He alone will bring

My Savior and King-my thirst for you unquenching

Your sacrifice heart wrenching

O resurrected King, You make my heart sing

The wonders of what You have done

Wash over me and through

My tears are stirred by the sights and sounds of all You have done

By Your goodness and mercy I am overcome

By Your grace and glory I am undone

Revere His holy name, remember why He came

Let the Spirit dance and the heart sing

Remember with gladness that He will reign

Remember the peace and prosperity that He will bring

Death and sin thrown down, life and peace with God abound

O resurrected King, You make my heart sing.

LYNN KRAJCI

YOUR GREATNESS THEY DECLARE

Lord, to what can you be compared?

To nothing; though Your greatness they declare.

A perfect raindrop resting on the petal of a rose?

Or gently falling winter snow?

10,000 butterflies floating on the wind?

Or the alluring fragrance of a flower when spring begins?

To the rising sun spewing colors across the sky?

Or perhaps a newborn baby's cry?

To none of these can You be compared

Though Your greatness Lord, they do declare

And to what can I compare Your love?

To a lion's roar or an antelope's leap?

A pollinating bee or a bird of prey soaring free?

Lord, Your love is more beautiful than all these.

More lovely than 10,000 butterflies floating on the breeze

Prettier than a perfect raindrop resting on the petal of a rose

Or gently falling winter snow

Oh, to what can You be weighed against?

There is no beauty or splendor so intense.

The intricate weaving of a spider's web?

Or a glorious eagle with its grand wings spread?

Though their beauty is plain to see

They are but a reflection of the love of the One

Who came to live and die to set us free

His resurrection is life

And His love and sacrifice

Will forever be my heart's delight.

No, to none of these can You be compared

Though Your greatness Lord, they do declare.

LYNN KRAJCI

NASB Romans 1:19-20 because that which is known about God is evident [b]within them; for God made it evident to them. For since the creation of the world His invisible *attributes, that is*, His eternal power and divine nature, have been clearly perceived, being understood by what has been made, so that they are without excuse.

YOUR LOVE

Your love like the ocean, vast and deep
Causes my very soul to weep

You are the awe in my heart
You are the song of my soul

Like winter chases the spring
Your loves chases my innermost being

Like the sun's warmth after a cold rain
You comfort me and keep me singing the same refrain

You are the awe in my heart
You are the song of my soul

Like an explosion of color when autumn bursts through
Your love stirs me with each morning new

Like a sea of daylilies dancing in the sun
Your love makes me feel like my life's just begun

As the sparrow's song faithfully comes with each new dawn
Your love faithfully and lavishly adorns

You are the awe in my heart
You are the song of my soul

You are the Ancient of Days, it's all Your plan
You who hold the universe in Your hands
You are my Lord and King
You are the God of everything

And Your love is the awe in my heart
Your love is the song of my soul

Your love like the oceans vast and deep
Causes my very soul to weep
Like winter chases spring
Your love chases my innermost being

Like the warmth of the sun after a cold rain
Your love comforts me and keeps me singing the same refrain

Your love is the awe in my heart
And Your love is the song of my soul.

LYNN KRAJCI

BECAUSE I SAID SO

Why do the stars shine in the sky?

Why do such lovely birds fly?

And the Lord let me know,

"Because I said so."

Why is the sunset so beautiful?

Why is a rainbow in the heavens so colorful?

And the Lord let me know,

"Because I said so."

Why is man redeemed by the Innocent One?

Father why did you send your perfect Son?

Why do His actions save the lost?

Why does His death pay the cost?

And the Lord crowed, "Because I said so!"

Why does His death and resurrection redeem?

Why does He restore and why does He intervene?

The wages of sin are death

And yet, why are we so blessed?

And He let me know,

"Because I said so!"

"Lord," I said, "I'm glad that You came

And I'm glad that You are always the same

The last and great authority

The standard for morality

The Everlasting, the never passing

Our glorious God and King."

But most of all I will sing

Because of what I am grateful to know

About the Lord who continues to crow,

"Because I said so!"

LYNN KRAJCI

NASB Romans 6:23 For the wages of sin is death, but the gracious gift of God is eternal life in Christ Jesus our Lord.

NASB 1 Peter1:18-19 knowing that you were not [a]redeemed with perishable things like silver or gold from your futile way of life inherited from your forefathers, but with precious blood, as of a lamb unblemished and spotless, *the blood* of Christ.

FOR WHAT REASON WERE YOU SAVED?

For what reason were you saved?

Were you the greatest or the one who was the bravest?

Were you the most humble or perhaps the most noble?

If so, for none of these were you saved

Were you the quickest, the smartest or the slickest?

Have you been a most reliable friend?

Did you set the latest most popular trend?

Perhaps you are gone, martyred for your cause

And you thought for this reason you would get the Lord's applause

But all have sinned and fallen short

All are condemned in the heavenly courts

You are saved by a gift of grace

And it is this grace that you ought to embrace

It is nothing you have done

You were saved by the selfless acts of the perfect Son

You were saved because He is great, merciful and true

You were saved because He cared for someone as pitiful as you

You were saved because He cares for the weak and the base

There is nothing good in you, not a single trace

But He wasn't seeking the great and wise

It was the foolish who caught His compassionate eyes

So, give up your pride, lay your crown at His feet

For Christ alone is worthy to take the royal seat

And be grateful that it does not depend on us

For on this you can trust

We would fail

If we were weighed on the heavenly scale

So be thankful to our Savior and King

Who did it all for us, so that we might sing

On the day of our salvation

"Glory to the God of all creation!

The God of grace and mercy!

The God holy and praiseworthy!

The Savior of the lost!

The One who endured the cross!

For He saves from every nation!

And He alone is the reason for our salvation!"

LYNN KRAJCI

NASB Romans 3:23 for all have sinned and fall short of the glory of God,

THE SILENT SOUND IN HEAVEN

If a prayer is heard and a prayer is blessed

With one voice alone, then what of the rest?

What of ten thousand entreating the King

Silently praying over a single thing?

Multiple voices beseeching the Lord

Praying and pleading with one accord

Praying in quiet adulation as we bend or kneel

Making our request, stating our appeal

If He answers the prayers of the humble and small

What might He do to answer us all?

If a prayer is heard and a prayer is blessed

For one voice alone, then what of the rest?

What of ten thousand entreating the King?

What of a myriad in unison over a single thing?

Ten thousand hearts in quiet worship and praise

O the silent sound in heaven our voices would raise!

LYNN KRAJCI

THE SONG OF MY SOUL

I won't let myself obey until I'm broken

My mind is untamed and unopen

Though Your righteous promises be true

I still plead my case against You

I try to resist

I stand and shake my fists

But You keep playing that irresistible cord

Which reveals Your mysterious wisdom Lord

I continue to drift away

And I won't be easily swayed

I'm refusing to embrace the bliss

Which comes through Your holy kiss

And still, I hear You playing the melody of my soul

Though I find it hard to hear from so far below

I continue to resist

And to shake my furious fists

I will not remain within Your gates

I'm still planning my grand escape

But You keep playing that holy chord

While I keep hurling my hate filled scorn

And I refuse to accept the kiss

That comes from Your holy lips

I deny that beautiful chord

That You tenderly play for me Lord

But You keep singing the song of my soul

And I fear I'm beginning to fold

And I'm still running as fast as I can

But it's getting harder and harder to stand

I won't give in unless I'm broken

But I'm crumbling now, I fear I'm chokin'

And I find that I want to stay

And I find I want to hear You play

The music of my soul

And I know that You won't let me go

Though I cover my ears from that beautiful sound

Because it's too lovely, it's too profound

Then suddenly I am humbled

By the truth that's making me crumble

I'm on my knees and I'm broken

By the Word that You have spoken

--That irresistible chord

--That You keep playing my Lord

The music of Your heart

That is the Word which You impart

By that Word You entreat

And by that Word You defeat

And now I sit below

Listening to the melody of my soul

Listening to that irresistible chord

That You so willingly play for me Lord

You keep singing the song of my soul

And I know, you won't let me go

You will not compromise

And so now I harmonize

You're singing Your holy song

And now I joyfully sing along

LYNN KRAJCI

TRUST HIM

When people let you down
And life thrusts you to the ground
When sorrow comes in waves of grief
And there seems to be
No help in reach

Trust Him.

When everything has changed
In ways that cause deep pain
Your existence is the enemy
And your losses leave you empty

Trust Him.

He is closer than any human friend
He will not abandon or contend
But will surely comfort and defend

If you'll only trust in Him.

Aching will be eased
And sadness turned to peace
The hollowness you feel inside will cease

As long as you trust in Him.

Trust Him, for He is the Christ of God, the Savior and King

To whom we confess, we can say no less, "We owe You everything!"

He will wipe away all tears

He will take away all pain

He will do away with fear

And eliminate all shame

Trust Him.

He is tender, yet He is strong

And friends it won't be long

Til we see Him coming in the clouds

And we'll praise Him and we'll shout,

"Glory to the Lion, the Lamb of God, our King!"

Then we'll worship and we'll sing

"Trust Him!"

LYNN KRAJCI

NASB Mark 13:26 And then they will see THE SON OF MAN COMING IN CLOUDS with great power and glory.

EMBRACED BY HIS GRACE

My God loves the unlovely and unlovable

He forgives the unforgivable

Has done the unfathomable

And I am embraced by His grace.

I cry, "How is this possible

That a heart such as mine

Which was to sin so inclined

To be so tenderly touched by the divine?"

I was worthy to be discarded

A child of the darkness

I was snatched out of the night

To be bathed in His wonderful light

I am embraced by His grace.

My heart has changed

My mind's rearranged

Now a child of the King

Once unlovely and unlovable

I now have reason to sing

And I am embraced by His grace.

How is it possible, a heart such as mine

Once so sinfully inclined

Would be so tenderly touched

By the great King divine

Could be so compassionately embraced

By the Lord's glorious grace.

LYNN KRAJCI

O MAN

O man, where is your dignity? Where is your worth?

How is it that you have come to live on the earth?

Who has formed you of the dust of the ground?

Why in your heart does such foolishness abound?

O man, how have you fallen so far from Him?

Do what is good, flee from your sin!

O man you are truly unique

Able to create, love, sing, and speak!

Were you not fearfully and wonderfully made?

Though you earned death, were you not saved?

Glorify, glorify, be true to your cause?

Know Him and love Him for whom you were born!

Find your dignity and crush your pride

You did not form yourself

It is in Him and for Him that you abide

Who is like you in this vast world O man?

Made in His image in dominion you stand

Blind to your reason for being

Requiring your eyes to be open for seeing

Your need for renewal, for redemption divine

Your need for mercy, forgiveness and rebirth sublime

O man where is your dignity? Where is your worth?

How is it that you have come to live on the earth?

Who has formed you of the dust of the ground?

Why in your heart does so much foolishness abound?

Were you not fearfully and wonderfully made?

Though you earned death, were you not saved?

Glorify your God, be true to your cause!

For this is the reason for which you were formed!

O man, where is your dignity? Where is your worth?

Made in God's image from your very birth.

LYNN KRAJCI

NASB Genesis 2:7 Then the LORD God formed the man of dust from the ground and breathed into his nostrils the breath of life; and the man became a living person.

NASB Psalm 139:14 I will praise You, for I am fearfully *and* wonderfully made; Marvelous are Your works, And *that* my soul knows very well.

NASB Genesis 1:27 So God created man in His own image, in the image of God He created him; male and female He created them

WHAT LOVE IS THIS

What love is this that renders all words inadequate?
A groom dies so that His bride might have life
Displaying great humility, it is the great sacrifice
Husband, faithful and unswerving
Wife, selfish and undeserving
What love is this?
Marked by scars of hands and feet
Marked by the enemies humiliating defeat
Unfaithful though she may be
He loves her still; He sets her free
What love is this that renders all words inadequate?
Words not suffice to say, nor enough time to find a way
To convey the heart of the One who gave His life for her
Though she unlovely be, He loves her still
Clearly, He adores her
She is weak and base and of little worth
Yet she He chose of all the earth
What love is this?
Marked by scars of hands and feet
Marked by death and death's defeat
Unfaithful though she may be
He loves her still; He sets her free
What love is this that renders all words inadequate?
It is a love of God's design
It is tenderness divine
Deep tenderness divine.

LYNN KRAJCI

SO BE IT, AMEN

Lord, I keep wondering why You are so willing,

To leave me feeling like I've got an empty soul.

And without You, there is nowhere in this world to go.

Lord, I keep wondering why,

Why You've left me with this heavy heart,

Taking those I love and letting them depart.

You've emptied my soul again,

And there's no consoling me within,

Because the place I've entered is too dark.

Lord, don't You even hear my screaming heart?

Why do You choose to rip my very soul apart?

Where has Your love hidden?

Why does Your love seem to be forbidden?

Without You there's nowhere to go.

And You've left me all alone with my empty soul.

You've turned off the sun to leave me groping in the dark.

Have You chosen to rip my very soul apart?

Lord, I'm wondering where You go,

And why You keep leaving me with this empty soul.

With trials upon trials tearing at me and wearing at me

Until finally, I drop down to my knees.

And there it is that I find You again.

There it is where my heart and soul You mend.

Then I see that it is I who left,

And You remained where You always are,

And I refused to see the light through the dark.

I dropped to my knees and there You reached for me,

Your gentle hand waiting for me to grab hold.

Oh, my Lord, there You were, waiting so long to console,

There You were waiting to carry my load,

There You took it from my so very tired soul.

When I dropped to my knees, I found You were there again,

And on my knees, my heart and soul You did mend.

Your tender hand waits for us to grab hold,

There Lord, you are willing to console,

And You are willing to take the weighty load off our souls,

If we will only have the sense,

To drop to our knees again.

And there You'll heal us; heart and soul You'll mend.

Oh Lord, when we will drop to our humble knees again,

And we say the words again;

Those sacred words, "So be it. Amen."

LYNN KRAJCI

THE OFFER: FOREVERMORE: A CONVERSATION WITH GOD

You say You will give us a new place to stay

Where there is peace

Where there is joy forevermore

But how can I reach it, grasp it to explore

Knowing only this world-rich in sorrow and pain?

You say You will give an endless life of gain

But how can I understand this life of utter bliss

When I have only known a life such as this

Where my sin drowns me in sorrow

With every tomorrow, my sin hems me in

It comes to accuse me again and again

But You say You offer a life better than this

A life that is sinless, a life that is bliss

A life free of troubles and sorrows

Not like the life we see with each new day

That returns with each unwelcome tomorrow

We live in a world of endless tears

That fills me with fears of living another day

And yet, You offer us endless tomorrows?

You say there is another way?

Not like this world, in that land of bliss

But I'm blinded by my own sin

And the sin of the world I'm living in

A world of poverty, greed, corruption and strife

A world whose ways cut like a knife

And You offer me something I cannot conceive

You offer that which is so hard to believe

Then I recall

I recall Your love

The love of the cross

Where we were bought

At a price so very high

And I am convinced

That You are the glorious Prince

Your offer is true, and so, my dear Lord are You

I see that the place You offer

Is the place where You live

And I'm beginning to understand

That there is such a land

Flowing with milk and honey

Lit by Your glory, sustained by Your power

Where hour by hour I long to be

This Prince will be the light of the place

When I look in His eyes I will see His grace

And the blood that soaked the cross

Was the love that paid the price

To that love I am drawn for it does surely entice

And so now I understand this eternal land You offer us

Is a truth that I can wholeheartedly trust

And I'm beginning to understand

That there is such a land

Flowing with milk and honey

Lit by Your glory, sustained by Your power

Where hour by hour, I long to be

The Prince will be the light of that place

And when I look in His eyes, I will see His grace

LYNN KRAJCI

NASB 1 Corinthians 6:20 For you have been bought for a price: therefore glorify God in your body.

NASB Exodus 3:8 So I have come down to rescue them from the power of the Egyptians, and to bring them up from that land to a good and spacious land, to a land flowing with mllk and honey,...

COME THE LORD'S DAY

Father why do tears from my eyes?

Why does everything cause me to cry?

Tragedy stands at my front and my back

And it's frightening to see all that the world seems to lack

People fight, people hate, and they strive

Few know the purpose for which they are alive

Few understand what Your Son has done

Sometimes there seems to be no way to cope

And so, few have found a reason to hope

Earthquakes abound, war is waging all around

The world is a powder keg, standing on one leg.

And so, I plead and so I beg

Minds are afflicted, hearts no longer sound

The world You made, a beautiful place, but sin surrounds

And there is no peace at the end of the day

And so, brethren, we must pray, "Come our Lord, come."

For to this world, we refuse to succumb

There is despair, joy is out of reach

You offer love, but it is the evil passions they seek

Father, please send the One

The One who took our place

The Almighty One who saves

He who fought our case

For we need Him to come

And to say once again, "It is finished, it is done."

O Father send Your one and only sacrificial Son

Our joy, the only hope of humanity

And stop this sinful insanity

Come our Lord; come and restore

Please Father, we painfully implore

And so, let it be the Lord's Day

And let it be the Lord's way. Come...

LYNN KRAJCI

THE LAMB'S BLOOD IS ON OUR DOORPOST

With the Lamb's blood on our doorposts

Death has passed us by

Predestined and unmerited we begin to cry,

"Glory to the Lamb! Praise to our King!

Who found it in His heart to do such wondrous things!"

Through the blood of the Lamb

We obtained the inheritance

So, we bow in devoted reverence

To the Lamb of God our King

Who decided with His love to such splendor bring

With the Lamb's blood on our doorposts

Death has passed us by

Predestined and unmerited we begin to sing,

"Glory to the Lamb! Praise to our King!

Who found it in His heart

To do such wondrous things."

Chosen in Him ere the foundation of the world

We feel a grand adoration

For the plan that He unfurled

Praise Him! Commend Him!

Applaud all that He has done!

Honor and exalt Him

Give Him glory 'til He comes

For with the Lamb's blood on our doorposts

Death has passed us by

And we begin to cry and sing,

"Glory to the Lamb of God

Shout praises to our King!"

Who found it in His heart

To such glorious splendor bring

Who found it in His love

To do such wondrous things

LYNN KRAJCI

NASB Exodus 12:3,7 12,13 ...take a ⌐lamb for themselves, according to the fathers' households, a lamb for each household. Moreover, they shall take some of the blood and put it on the two doorposts and on the lintel [1]of the houses in which they eat it. For I will go through the land of Egypt on that night, and fatally strike all the firstborn in the land of Egypt.. The blood shall be a sign for you on the houses where you ⌐live; and when I see the blood I will pass over you, and no plague will come upon you]to destroy *you* when I strike the land of Egypt.

TO LIVE IS CHRIST

For to me, to live is Christ, to die is gain

The question is raised

And the question is weighed

When there is pain, I consider it

And I remember this

The Lord is my master

And I know His answer

"Live!"

Live and obey

Live so you can say,

"Awake those who sleep!"

Shout it in the streets

Shout it from the highest heights

"Jesus Christ is King!"

So, praise Him for everything

Give glory to the Lord

Spread His name abroad

Let Him be known to everyone

Let His fame shine like the sun

I wish all the world could see

The love that He's shown me

To live is Christ, to die is gain

The question is raised

And the question is weighed

The Lord is my master

I know what He will answer,

"Live"

Live and obey

Live so you can pray

For all to know the love and hope of Christ

Let your words touch and entice

Join those who say,

"Take the long and narrow way,"

Then shout it in the streets

Awake those who sleep!

Shout it from the highest heights

Announce it every day and night

Praise to our Lord

Praise to our King

Praise Him for everything

And live, live for our Lord

Live for our King

Live to thank Him for everything

Let this be your practice

Share the reason for your gladness

And live.

LYNN KRAJCI

NASB Philippiansn 1:21 For to me, to live is Christ, and to die is gain.

THE GIFT

The grass is green and high, so that it blows in the wind

The mountains spread out in the distance

They appear a bluish-gray hue

And I smell the wildflowers' blooms

I stand in the shade of an ancient oak

I hear the song thrush's melodic notes

The sun rises, the sky is ablaze with color

I am stunned and stand in awestruck wonder

A crooked stream flows to one side

At this scene my fears suddenly fly

You made it Lord for our delight

These lovely sounds and lovely sights

I thank You for the ancient oak

For the song thrush's melodic notes

For the tall green grass that sways in the wind

And the bluish-gray mountains in the distance

For the wildflowers' blooms

And the sunset's dazzling hue

Lord, for all these things, I give thanks to You

A monarch butterfly comes floating by

And suddenly I begin to joyfully cry

Touched by the love I see in all this

For You gave me this moment of utter bliss

And I feel as though I have received a holy kiss

For I was given such an underserved gift

Then I recall that You shed Your blood

And I cannot comprehend such limitless love

I see the pretty day is just a taste

Of Your unbounding grace

And so, I place my true faith

In the God of such love

To which no other love can stand above

And I accept the gift immeasurable

Which is given through the Father and His Son

For I cannot turn away nor resist

The profound, groundless, boundless God-given gift.

LYNN KRAJCI

NASB Romans 6:23 …The gracious gift of God in is eternal life in Christ Jesus our Lord.

THE BOOK OF LIFE

Lord, do You know my name?

Is it written in Your Book of Life?

Did You bear my shame?

Did You suffer my plight?

The elect You claimed

When You endured the cross

In the fight that You fought

How I love You Lord

For the death that Your endured

But do You know my name?

Is it written in Your Book of Life?

I'll never be the same

Because You paid the price

You fought the great fight

And I know You came

To shine a great light

And to write my name

In Your Book of Life.

LYNN KRAJCI

NASB Isaiah 9:2 The people who walk in darkness will see a great light…

NASB Mark 13:20 …for the sake of the elect, whom He chose, He shortened the days.

NASB Philippians 4:3 …whose names are in the book of life.

HIS ALL

Be careful where you place your heart

For from this world you will surely depart

And there is no worthwhile thing that from this world you can ever bring

Everything good has been given to you

So, don't foolishly trust in riches and jewels

Turn from ungodly ways

To look to the Son and sing His praise

As one who trusts in his riches will fall

And the one who trusts in Him will gain all

The one who trusts in Him will not die

But will receive eternal life sublime

So, look to the Lord and give Him praise

Trust only in Him for the rest of your days

For the one who trusts in riches will fall

But the one who trusts in Him will gain all

Throw away the worthless things of this life

And accept the exquisite pearl of great price

Choose godliness, choose holiness-

Choose to follow the King

And lose it all to gain a good thing

Refuse the temporary joys

And evil worldly sinful ploys

Choose to follow the meaningful and lasting

Choose to lose the shallow and passing

In Christ a wonderful future awaits

It is in Him that I put my faith

For to me He beckons, to me He calls

So, I've given Him my heart, which is so small

While He has given to me, His all…

LYNN KRAJCI

NASB Matthew 13:46 …who, when he had found one pearl of great price, went and sold all that he had and bought it.

NASB 1 Timothy 6:7 For we have brought nothing into the world, so we cannot take anything out of it, either.

NASB Proverbs 11:28 One who trusts in his riches will fall…

Printed in the United States
by Baker & Taylor Publisher Services